HARDWICK OLD

DERBYSHIRE

Lucy Worsley
Assistant Inspector of Historic Buildings

Hardwick Old Hall was the family home of Bess of Hardwick, one of the most remarkable women of the Elizabethan age. A series of four marriages made her one of the richest women in England, and gave her the independence to embark on a series of grand building projects to display her wealth and authority. Confined to Hardwick as a result of a quarrel with her fourth husband, the Earl of Shrewsbury, she rebuilt the house in a grand and lavish style in the 1580s and 90s, before embarking on the more stupendous New Hall next door. By the eighteenth century, the hall was neglected and left to fall into decay.

This fully illustrated guidebook provides a tour of the house as it can be seen today, together with the story of Bess's life and history of the house, as well as giving a flavour of what life might have been like in the house's heyday.

❖ CONTENTS ❖

INTRODUCTION

TOUR OF THE HOUSE
6   *Exterior*
8   *Hall*
10 *Forest Great Chamber*
13 *Service areas*
13 *Up the stairs*
14 *The upper servants*
16 *Hill Great Chamber*
20 *Onto the leads*
20 *The tennis court*
22 *The west lodge*
22 *Conduit house*

HISTORY
23 *Bess of Hardwick*
24 *Hardwick before Bess*
26 *William Cavendish and William St Loe*
28 *Bess marries the Earl of Shrewsbury*
30 *War between the Earl and Countess*
33 *Bess's descendants*

Published by English Heritage
23 Savile Row, London W1X 1AB
© English Heritage 1998
First published by English Heritage 1998
Photographs, unless otherwise specified, were taken by English Heritage
Photographic Unit, and remain the copyright of English Heritage

Edited by Lorimer Poultney
Designed by Pauline Hull
Printed in England by Sterling Press
LP C80 4/98 FA3561 ISBN 1 85074 695 8

INTRODUCTION

'No curse or plague in the world could be more grievous', wrote the Earl of Shrewsbury in 1585. He was describing his wife Elizabeth, Countess of Shrewsbury – better known to us as 'Bess of Hardwick' and the builder of the Halls at Hardwick.

He claimed that she had spread evil reports about him and had always sought for her own interests. She was of so 'base a parentage' and so 'devilish a disposition' that he could not live with her. Although Queen Elizabeth herself demanded that the two be reconciled in her presence, nothing could mend their differences.

Bess (1527–1608) was one of the richest women in England, and the quarrel was over her money and lands. As a result of an extraordinary series of marriages, Bess had the power to leave her fourth and last husband, the Earl, and retire to her childhood home to build two great houses in the 1580s and 90s. She began building the New Hall even before the Old was finished.

Why are there two houses so close to each other on the hilltop? How was a woman able to commission such extraordinary architecture? Why is the Old Hall such an odd, jumbled building? The explanation lies in this violent sixteenth-century quarrel.

View of the north front of Hardwick Old Hall, with the lodges in the foreground

Cut-away reconstruction drawing by Philip Winton
of how the house may have looked in the early
seventeenth century

**Forest Great
Chamber**
pages 10–13
An important
room used
for formal
occasions,
dining and
entertainments

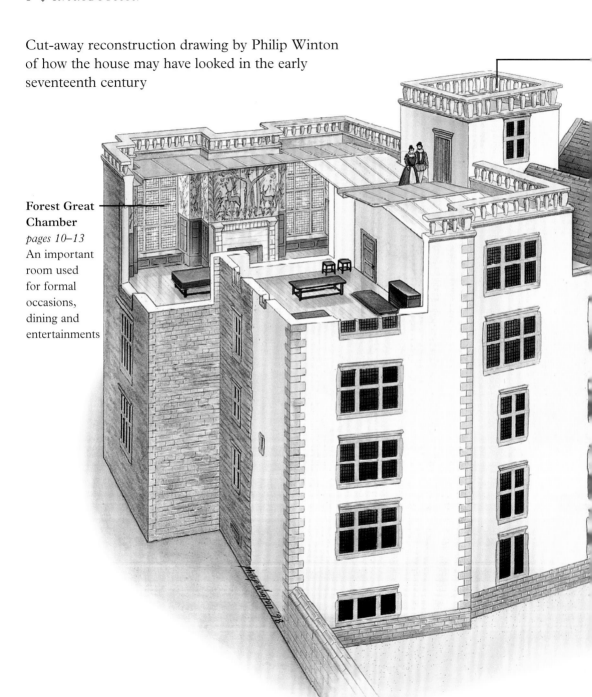

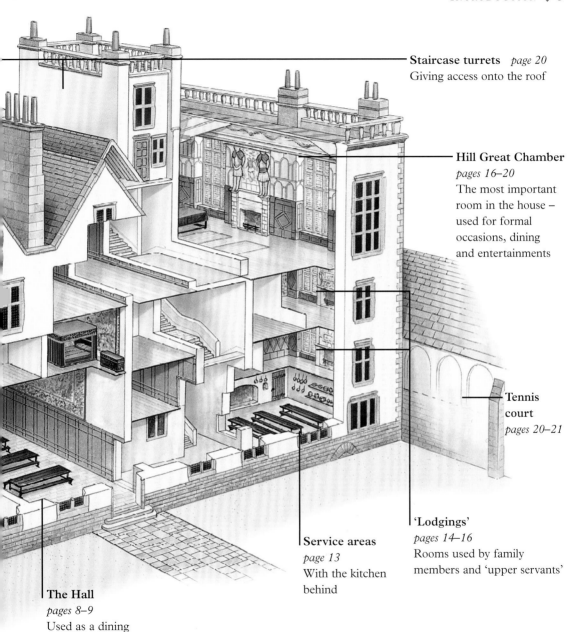

Staircase turrets *page 20*
Giving access onto the roof

Hill Great Chamber
pages 16–20
The most important
room in the house –
used for formal
occasions, dining
and entertainments

**Tennis
court**
pages 20–21

'Lodgings'
pages 14–16
Rooms used by family
members and 'upper servants'

Service areas
page 13
With the kitchen
behind

The Hall
pages 8–9
Used as a dining
room for the
'lower servants'

TOUR OF THE
HOUSE

Exterior

The tour starts at the display panel in front of the house. The drawing shows how the house would have looked from here when complete.

The house has clearly grown organically over time, and is not neat and symmetrical like the contrasting New Hall. This is because Bess added accommodation piecemeal and at speed after she was left homeless owing to the quarrel with her husband. She massively extended the old Hardwick house, one wall of which survives around the windows and fireplace in the hall. The east wing may also be based on an earlier building, as it does not line up with the hall.

The result was an imperfect and inconvenient house, but the work done here was a trial run for her great project across the way. For example, you can see the inspiration for the New Hall in the enormous rectangular windows of the Great Chambers in the two wings of the Old Hall. Their sharp, rectangular

Seventeenth–century drawing showing how the building looked when still complete

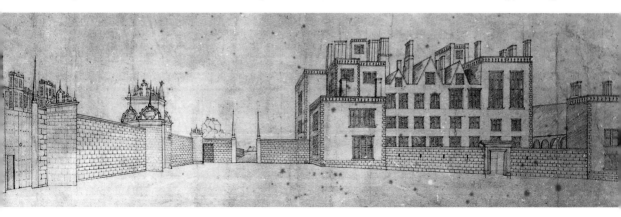

❖ BUILDING HARDWICK ❖

Account books for the Hardwick estate survive and give many details about the expenses of Bess's household, from the cost of building materials to the food eaten. Because the two houses, the Old Hall and the New, were run as one home, the accounts rarely distinguish between money spent at one and at the other. Also, Bess spent much of her time at other estates, such as Chatsworth. Her household was like a small court moving round a kingdom. Much of our information about Hardwick comes from these records.

Very detailed accounts of Bess's building work survive. Her overseer made them up every two weeks and Bess checked them personally. She signed each page 'E Shrousbury' (meaning Shrewsbury), and often corrected his mistakes.

❖ In 1583, Bess bought the Hardwick estate, including the older house in which she was born (remnants of which survive in the south and west walls of the hall), on the death of her brother James. In 1584, she had to leave Chatsworth. The Earl was harassing her and her tenants.

❖ By 1587, Bess's income was assured by a legal decision and she had the confidence to start building. When the accounts begin, she had already extended the existing hall. That year saw work on three floors of the east wing, including the third floor gallery and Bess's own suite of rooms, which were finished, gabled and slate-roofed by the end of the year.

❖ In 1588, the four floors of the west wing were thrown up, incorporating a room called 'my ladies old bed chamber', which was also perhaps part of the earlier house. The Hill Great Chamber was part of this phase. Also in 1588, the central hall block was heightened by an extra storey and a great gable built.

❖ In 1589, the workmen also went back to the east wing and built the Forest Great Chamber at the top, in smooth ashlar stone unlike the rough-cast used previously. They added an inner shell to the south wall of the east wing to provide strength to carry the new top floor. The main stairs off the hall were rebuilt, and they led up to a turret providing access to the east wing roof.

Work continued on and off for the next seven years, but now the New Hall was the focus of the builders' efforts.

The south front, looking east towards the east wing

outlines hint at the New Hall's stark towers.

Why did Bess build these two houses so close together? The answer is that she needed both of them to shelter her large household. In 1590, before the Old Hall was finished, her workmen were already digging the foundations of the New Hall. The New Hall, after all, was only to have a few grand bedrooms, and Bess often had sixty or seventy people to house.

The two lodges behind you were added at later stage, perhaps in a rather careless effort to smarten up the Old Hall by making it look more symmetrical from the outside. The lodge on the left has been conserved as a shop and education rooms. The eastern, plastered lodge houses English Heritage staff. Both lodges and the hall were once plastered. The original road to the Hall came up from the west, sweeping round what is now the wooded hillside.

Hall

Now go into the porch.

This seems to have been built or rebuilt in the early twentieth century. You can see just inside on the left, under the window, that it has been made re-using what seem to be old gravestones. One is apparently dated 1904.

Go in through the existing door-way, which has been made out of a window. The hall fireplace is decorated with an enormous plaster stag, Bess's emblem. This is a most unusual room because its long axis stretches away into the depth of the building. Nearly all other halls before this stretched sideways across a building – and you would always come in from the outside through a door in the long side of the hall, not the short end, as we are doing here.

This is an 'end-on' hall, like the one Sir Christopher Hatton had already experimented with in the little lodge at his splendid palace at Holdenby. But in the case of Hardwick this hall only became 'end-on' by accident. The hall may well have been part of the earlier house, and was entered from the long east side. The extension of the house swallowed it up, and the original outside entrance on the long side, now missing, became internal. The door and porch at the end were the logical conclusion to having the hall 'end-on'. If you visit the New Hall, you can see that Bess was so taken with her innovation that she repeated it over there. But the new 'end-on' hall always had its door at the short end, not the long side.

Meals would be brought in through the doorway to your right. The important end was up by the fireplace, where the high table was. But Bess and her family would not have eaten there themselves like medieval lords. They ate in the Great Chambers upstairs, or in the 'low dining chamber' on more private occasions, or even in their bedrooms. Lady Anne Clifford, another great builder, kept a diary, and wrote for the 28 December 1616, that 'I dined above in my Chamber & wore my Night Gown because I was not very well.'

Still, all the lower servants ate in the hall, and there would have been complaints about the noise they made. Households like Bess's were so huge that they needed a special book of rules, called 'books of orders', and one such book tells us how the steward would enter with his stick, shouting 'softly, my masters'.

Explore the service room through the door nearest the fireplace. This room was used for storing and serving the beer everyone drank with their meals. Usually it was kept in a dark cellar underground, but the building has no cellar. If you look high up on the west wall, you can see the remains of a plaster fireplace with Bess's emblem of stags, and a motto, which read:
'As fainting stags the water requireth, Even so my soul the Lord desireth.'

Engraving of the south front, 1799

European Magazine.

Old Hardwick Nottinghamshire, the Seat of the Duke of Devonshire.

J. P. Malcolm del. et f

Publish'd by J. Sewell Cornhill Jan.ʸ 1ˢᵗ 1799.

❖ UPPER AND LOWER SERVANTS ❖

At midsummer 1597, Bess had 74 servants on the books, many of whom were her own relations. These servants were divided between 'upper' servants, who were of good families and had responsible jobs, and 'lower' servants, who did more menial tasks.

The women were especially important in this household, and the five who top the list were the gentlewomen who were Bess's companions. Bess herself had served in a similar role in the households of Lady Zouche, Lady Dorset and then Queen Elizabeth. The upper gentlemen servants had business roles; Sir Henry Jenkinson, a clergyman, paid out the building expenses, Mr Reason collected rent, and kept the money in an iron chest with two locks, bands and hasps. Timothy Pusey, known simply as Timothy, was in a position of great trust and was often sent shopping in London or to arrange legal matters.

We know some of the lower servants' jobs, too. There was a gardener, who was bought a new spade and twelve fruit trees in 1597, a scullery man and a foot boy. All the servants, upper and lower, wore a uniform. In 1597 Bess bought 'mallard' colour cloth to make 35 'livery cloaks', as they were called, and 'blewe cloath' for coats for 34 others. She paid for the keeping of one of their sons at school. She made a gift of money at the christening of Stanley the cook's baby.

She made a long list of gifts at New Year, starting with a very expensive one to the queen, large sums of money to her children, and smaller sums to other members of the household. New Year was present-giving time. But at Christmas in 1597 two barrels of oysters were eaten and thirteen paupers were given a 'dishe of meat' on each of the twelve days of the holiday.

This was probably in what was once the Little Gallery. Abraham the joiner was bought 200 nails in 1599 for making a 'Cubbord' for this room.

Forest Great Chamber

The floorless room with huge windows at the top of the east wing is the Forest Great Chamber. Surprisingly, there are two Great Chambers at the Old Hall. Possibly one was for Bess, and one for grand visitors. Both Chatsworth and Worksop Manor, the house of Bess's husband, also had double great suites.

A more likely reason in this case was that Bess's son William was living with her, and he needed his own rooms in the west wing. He was her second son by her favourite husband, Sir William Cavendish. Her eldest son, whom she called 'my bad son Henry', was to inherit Chatsworth, and had no legitimate heirs. Bess, intending to found a dynasty, built Hardwick up for William, who later became the 1st Earl of Devonshire. His descendants, the Dukes of Devonshire, inherited both Chatsworth and Hardwick, and it was the 10th Duke who gave Hardwick to the nation in 1959.

Bess's visitors reached the Great Chamber by the 'great stairs'. Their remains are to the left of the fire-place end of the hall. The grander the stairs, the grander the owner of the house. Lord Cecil wrote of Holdenby, another great Elizabethan house, that he was impressed by 'your stately ascent from your hall to your great chamber, and your cham-ber answerable with largeness and

A drawing of the plaster 'forest folk' in the Forest Great Chamber

❖ BESS'S CRAFTSMEN ❖

The account books tell us about the workmen who built the hall. Abraham Smith, the plasterer of the trees in the Forest Great Chamber, had also worked for Bess at Chatsworth, and remained in her service until she died. So did Thomas Accres, a skilled marble mason, highly paid, who had worked at Chatsworth for Bess in 1576, went to work at Wollaton Hall, and came back

to Bess at Hardwick in 1595. He had a 'boye' or apprentice called Luke Dolphin.

Craftsmen often worked by 'bargains' or piecework, undertaking a certain job for a certain sum. Ralph Smith, a carpenter, had to mortgage his house to Bess for failing to keep the bargain he 'should have done' in 1589.

The man who oversaw these 'bargains', and who also

decided many of the designs, was John Ballechouse, some-times called John Painter in the accounts, because of his difficult name. Perhaps origi-nally from Tours, he may have brought many up-to-date Flemish patterns to Bess. He was important enough to have his own room in the Old Hall in 1591, and to build the house which is now the Hardwick Inn at the bottom of the hill.

❖ MEALS AND BANQUETS ❖

Most of the food eaten in the Halls came directly from the estate and groceries were bought with a weekly payment not broken down in the accounts. But special items were recorded individually. Bess's servant Timothy was sent to London for foreign luxuries: pepper, ginger, cinnamon, preserved nutmegs, sugar loaves (an expensive import), currants and linseed oil. Cheese, capons, larks and peascods were brought from neighbours. Rosemary was sent over by Bess's daughter Grace and pigeons by her son-in-law Mr Pierrepont. Fish came from further afield: red herrings and sprats from Mansfield. Being so far away from the coast, the fish was not always very fresh, and the Earl of Shrewsbury wrote to Bess in 1575 that he had been sick all night after eating her-rings! In the summer Mr Manners sent strawberries over weekly.

For the dessert after the afternoon dinner, there were musk comfits (sweets), sweet fennel comfits, caraway com-fits and white sugar candy, or French prunes and Damask prunes from the Middle East. This course could be eaten in another room or 'banqueting house'. Wine was bought in huge volumes; for example, 2 hogsheads of 'Clarett' on 22 August 1598, along with 8 gallons of vinegar and a bottle of the sweet wine called sack.

lightsomeness.' And Bess could have seen this for herself when she visited Holdenby in 1592.

Business visitors may have been received in a room on the second or third floor, but important guests would have to climb right up to the top. Bess had unusually tall houses, with fourth floor Great Chambers. Food for meals would also make the journey up all these stairs, carried by a formal procession of servants.

The Forest Great Chamber takes its name from the plaster decorations of 'forest folk' – the deer prancing among the trees – perhaps inspired by decoration at Theobalds, another great Elizabethan house. The trees were made to look realistic by plas-tering around real tree trunks and branches. You may be able to make out the scene of deer, trees and behind them a door.

Perhaps Bess was making a spe-cial point here: she had quarrelled with her husband, but was quite ready for his apology and would then return to live with him. The deer, Bess's emblems, are waiting among the oak trees, symbols of constancy, to be invited back inside the door of her husband's house.

Bess also used the forest theme around the top of her Great Chamber in the New Hall, where you will see it is still colourfully painted. Behaviour was very formal in the Great Chamber, the most important room in the house. Another book of orders describes how 'in that place there must be no delay, because it is the place of state, where the lord keepeth his presence.'

So much of the east wing is missing that its internal plan is unclear. The demolition happened in the eighteenth century when the Dukes of Devonshire came to prefer their great new house at Chatsworth, and the materials were sold off.

Service areas

The second door off the hall, nearer the porch, goes into the kitchen area. Its lobby has a serving hatch like a window through to the kitchen beyond. This was the start of the procession that Bess's meals made upstairs. Inside the kitchen, there is a great fireplace where meat was roasted on a spit, and the lesser fireplace in the corner. If you look up the west wall to the room above, the nursery, you may be able to make out the plaster overmantel. It shows a scene from the biblical story of Tobias, a great favourite of Bess's. 'Tobie', as Bess called him, is setting out on a journey. The plaster scene was taken from a Flemish engraving, the caption of which gives the secret of the subject.

Through the door right of the fireplace you can turn left and left

again into the Pastry. This was a room for baking, and the huge fireplace contains several deep bread ovens. The little cellar room next to it was a larder.

Up the stairs

Now go back to the lobby outside the kitchen.

Less important than the great stair, this staircase is more important architecturally. Looking up it, you can see how the flights double back on themselves. Older staircases went up in either a spiral, or round a central newel post like in the grand stair off the hall. This innovatory

The fireplace in the Pastry, with ovens for baking

Looking up the staircase

Plaster overmantel in Mr Reason's room. William Reason, whose wages were £10 per year, was the receiver of rents.

Flemish engraving of Aser, from a set of The Twelve Patriarchs, which provided the inspiration for the subject

FITZWILLIAM MUSEUM, CAMBRIDGE

Plaster overmantel in Mr Digby's room, with a figure representing Air surrounded by the winds

doubling-back is yet another feature that Bess took across to the New Hall.

Up the stairs, round the bend and through the doorway to your left, are what were once William Cavendish's own rooms. The plaster overmantel shows a figure astride yet another stag. Another engraving tells us that he is Naphtali, one of the biblical patriarchs. Although the rooms are large and had a good view, their position was poor as they were right over the pastry. Inadequate accommodation for her son was another reason why Bess needed to build the New Hall.

At the next opening, you can see a stack of blocked doorways on four different floors. They led out to a separate tower, perhaps containing the 'garderobes' or toilets, at a hygienic distance from the bedrooms. This was perhaps added after Bess's time, as there is no mention of it in the building accounts. Bess herself used a 'close stool' as a toilet. This was a wooden seat with a chamber pot inside, and 'covered with blue cloth stitched with white, with red and black fringe'.

The upper servants

Upstairs round the next bend are two rooms together on the left with plaster overmantels. These are the rooms of Mr Digby and Mr Reason, two of the upper servants. The blocked door between them shows the position of a passage over the hall linking the wings.

Mr Digby's overmantel, on the right, is a personification of Air, with the winds blowing about him. It was one of a series of Earth, Air, Fire and Water. Mr Digby's wife was the best-paid of all Bess's servants, and the daughter of Bess's half-sister. He later became a knight and sheriff of

❖ EMBROIDERY ❖

Bess and her ladies passed much of their time doing needlework. Used in furnishing and clothing, many pieces can still be seen across the way in the New Hall. There was a professional male 'imbroderer' on the staff to help with large projects, and many payments were made for taffeta, silk, canvas and fustian. Some materials were for making clothes: buttons, green keirsie for a jerkin, garters, a girdle, shoes, a hat, damask for a gown, lace for another, with whale bone for support and Venice gold for decoration.

Bess had her estates and business to attend to as well as her needlework, but life for many other aristocratic women was very empty. Mary, Queen of Scots, when held in captivity by the Earl of Shrewsbury, spent her days embroidering. Lady Anne Clifford, who later inherited land and found employment in building like Bess, complained of boredom in her diary. In April, 1617, she wrote 'The 31st I sat still thinking the time to be very tedious.'

Detail of a wall-hanging in the New Hall showing Penelope, one of Bess's favourite classical heroines

Derbyshire. Mr Reason's room, on the left, has a plaster overmantel of a man milking a goat, an image taken from an engraving of a biblical figure, Aser.

The reasonably high status of these rooms is revealed by the opulent furnishings described in an inventory (a list of contents) from 1601. Mr Manners, another relation, had a room next door with 'five pieces of tapestry hangings with personages, nine feet deep, a bedstead with head and posts turned, a tester and bedshead of blue cloth stitched with white and single vallans with a blue and white silk fringe, five curtains of blue cloth stitched with white, a counterpane of red and yellow Capha [a rich silk cloth]'.

But this was nothing compared to the 'Best Bedchamber' in the east wing, which had 'a bedstead with head and posts gilt and inlaid, a tester of murry and tawny velvet embroidered with double vallans fringed with gold and murry silk, the tester and bedshead having arms embroidered in them, five curtains of red and yellow silk damask trimmed with gold and red silk lace, a counterpane of cloth of gold and purple satin script, a mattress, a down bed, a diaper quilt, a bolster, two pillows, a pair of fusteans, a Spanish blanket', and much other furniture.

Opposite us are 'the corner chamber over Mr Wm Cavendish', and to the right, the 'Corner Chamber next the court.' Both had an inner chamber or lobby, where a servant might have slept. Of course, there was much less desire for privacy in Bess's house than we expect. One reason why beds had curtains was to screen the sleeper from people passing through bedrooms. Corridors were not yet normal.

Hill Great Chamber

Finally, on the top floor lies the splendid Hill Great Chamber. This room, although lacking its roof and floor, still gives some idea of its former splendour. When intact, this room must have been even more impressive than the High Great Chamber in the New Hall because of the clear view on three sides. It was important for a great landowner to see from, and be seen in, his great house with its large windows. One Elizabethan writer described how 'each one desireth to set his house aloft on the hill, to be seen far off, and cast forth his beames of stately and curious workmanship into every quarter of the country.' But this description also shows how unusual Bess's buildings were for the time. The 'curious work-

manship' much admired usually consisted of all sorts of extra decoration plastered onto the building, such as pediments, little niches, statues and decorative panels. Bess's buildings at Hardwick are quite plain and clean and stark in their rectangular outline, as you can see more clearly at the New Hall. In a way, they are curiously like modern skyscrapers. This was

Above right: 'The Triumph of Patience', a Flemish engraving from a set published in 1559 and the inspiration for the figure of 'Desire' in the centre of the overmantel

Below right: The fireplace in the Hill Great Chamber, with its splendid overmantel

one of the individual marks of her architect, Robert Smythson.

This room is often called the 'Giants' Chamber' because of the giant figures over the fireplace, who are perhaps Gog and Magog. The winged figure between them is 'Desire'. He was copied from an engraving after van Heemskerck, which shows Desire and Hope lead-ing Patience on a triumphal chariot, with Fortune shackled behind in disgrace. This can also be read as a comment on Bess's situation. She is Patience, who desires to triumph over the iniquities of her husband, and defeat cruel Fortune who had put so many obstacles in her way. But this message was hidden unless you held the key of the full engraved scene.

Reconstruction drawing by Peter Urmston of Bess dining in the Hill Great Chamber

❖ DINING AND MASQUING ❖

The Hill Great Chamber was used for dining and dancing for the family, important servants and honoured guests. The Elizabethan writer Whetstone imagined a party in such a Great Chamber. It was 'attired like a second paradise: the earthly Goddesses, in brightness, resembled heavenly creatures… the sweet music recorded the harmony of angels, the strange and curious devices in masquers seemed to be figures of divine mysteries… the very place was like an imagined Paradise.' These 'goddesses' and 'angels' were just his friends, dressed up to perform a masque, a danced entertainment. Aristocrats would watch or take part in masques on special occasions after dinner. Bess often listened to music. She would hear John

Manuscript of a song from the collection of William Cavendish, Bess's grandson

Briggs her trumpeter playing, or Mr Starky and Mr Parker singing. She made payments to other musicians; those of Mr Henry Cavendish, the Earl of Rutland and the Earl of Essex. She wrote to make sure her daughter Frances practised the virginal, a keyboard instrument, while she was away, and bought a set of viols for her grand-daughter Arbella. There are payments in the accounts to 'those that played at ye drawing chamber door' and on one occasion there is a glimpse of some more formal entertainment: she paid musicians and 'those that built the bower', perhaps a kind of stage set. To entertain the household, a bear was once brought to Chatsworth!

Opposite: Masquers entertaining diners at a banquet: detail from the funerary picture of Sir Henry Unton

Bess often used stories like this to project her image as a virtuous wife, and was fond of the classical heroines Lucretia and Penelope, who were both famously faithful to their husbands in adversity.

From the windows you can see across Bess's territory. To the north lay Sheffield Manor, one of her

husband's houses, and Bolsover Castle, house of her son Charles. Nearby was Oldcotes, the house she later built for William. It too seems to have been designed by Robert Smythson, probable designer of her new Hall at Hardwick. Beyond hills to the west was Chatsworth, which she had built and then left after the quarrel with

The Hill Great Chamber today

Onto the leads

While climbing the final flight of stairs, notice how higher up the stairs curve away from you round the bend. This is another feature of the stairs in the New Hall, perhaps inspired by this little flight. Lady Anne Clifford, whose diary we mentioned before, described her daily routine in 1616. 'I…used to arise betime in the morning, & walk upon the Leads and afterwards hear Reading.' By 'the leads' she meant that she took her exercise on the leaded roof of her house. This staircase led to the flat leaded roof of the west wing. Here Bess could walk in safety, protected by the balustrade, of which a fragment remains, or watch distant huntsmen chasing deer through the park. Hunts were often carried out with the pleasure of spectators in mind.

The tennis court

Go back down the stairs, and leave the west wing through the kitchen. Go out of the door into the service courtyard.

The little buildings out here in 1601 included a bakehouse, brewhouse, wash-house, dairy, slaughterhouse, stable and smithy. There was also a chandler's house for making candles, and a still house, fitted with stills, for distilling cordials for use in desserts, medicine or scent. These all show how important the yard was to the functioning of Bess's home. There

Shrewsbury, and to the south was his manor at South Wingfield.

As a great landowner, Bess had responsibilities to the people living nearby. Payments of money were 'geven to the poore about Hardwicke' every single week, and the amounts rose in times of bad harvest. This was not just generosity; it was a matter of prestige for the wealthy to be hospitable. Money was given 'to some pore folke at my going and coming from Oulecotes', which meant that she was distributing alms along the way to the other house at Oldcotes. Subsidies were also made 'to a pore woman that brought cakes', and to 'an old harpur' (an old harp-player).

were beds, too, in many of these rooms, including in Mr Cavendish's own stable. The numerous servants had to pack themselves in wherever possible.

The yard, curiously, was later converted into a tennis court. Perhaps this was done to celebrate the visit of the young prince Charles Stuart in 1619, a keen player. Robert Smythson's son John, also a designer of buildings, was paid nearly £650 for work to the Old Hall at this time, so the design of the court could well be his. It was not for playing modern tennis, but for 'real' or 'royal' tennis, which was played indoors against a wall, like a mixture of modern squash and badminton. If you look at the reconstruction drawing on pages 4–5, you can see the arcaded tennis court to the right.

The tennis court was maintained throughout the seventeenth century. Because it was set into the hillside below the level of the courtyard, gutters had to be built in 1663 to prevent water from flooding it. The nets and pulleys were repaired, the roof unmossed, the floor was sometimes blanched and red marks and figures re-made upon it. Other markings were made of 'black earth', perhaps coal dust, brought from the park at Wollaton.

A game of 'real' tennis in progress at Hampton Court, one of the few surviving real tennis courts

Paint research has revealed how the lodge was decorated, including a bright, garish Victorian period and a wallpapered twentieth century. Surviving fragments are displayed in the shop. This picture is a photomicrograph, a magnification of a tiny sample of the paint layers from the skirting board in the hallway.

The west lodge

The way out also goes back through the lodge. Above, there are four rooms used as lodgings or bedsits by servants. It was inhabited up to 1959 by the Duke of Devonshire's agent, and latterly used by English Heritage's workmen, but at some point in the eighteenth century it was perhaps abandoned. There is a lot of graffiti hidden under the paint, including dates and curious cabalistic circles.

The kitchen, or present shop, had cupboards decorated with 'graining': wood painted brown with an imitation grain. This was renewed no less than 12 times. Even the stone mullions of the window were also 'grained'. The shop also has a lead sink still set into the window sill, hidden under a flap, as a reminder of its former domestic use.

In 1996–97 the lodge had its roof releaded and decayed structural stonework was replaced. You can new stone mainly around the windows. The floors and partition walls were replaced, but the original materials, including many of the doors and the glass in the windows, were reused as far as possible. The floors are made of limeash, a traditional form of concrete made without cement.

Conduit house

If you walk around the outside of the Hall to the south front, you will see the little arched conduit house where water was stored. It was pumped up by an iron wheel turned by the 'water horse' in a lost wellhouse. The water ran along a lead channel from the conduit into the kitchen area.

Photograph of the front of the hall, taken by Richard Keene of Derby c.1860–65

HISTORY

❖

Bess of Hardwick

The story of Bess's life is not quite a tale of rags to riches, but she did start from relatively humble beginnings in a minor gentry family. She rose to become a 'costly countess' who was a friend of the Queen, and who built some of the most remarkable houses of her age.

Bess is famous for marrying four husbands. Marriage was the only career available to well-born Elizabethan women, and could be a path to social advancement. Bess gained enormous wealth through her marriages and the deaths of subsequent husbands, and this gave her the power finally to resist her last husband and live an unusually independent life.

The fact that the queen herself was a woman seemed very odd to people, an inversion of the normal order of things. This is why Elizabeth had to declare that although she had a weak woman's body, she had the 'heart and stomach of a king.' One reason that Bess aroused such resentment and fear was, simply, that she was a woman, and it seemed unnatural for anyone, particularly an earl, to submit to her. This resentment has survived in historical accounts of Bess that describe her as very hard and vicious; she was drawn in 1790 as 'a woman of masculine understanding and conduct, proud, furious, selfish and unfeeling.' Even one of her descendants described her in 1845 as 'hideous, dry, parched, narrow-minded… prudent, amassing and calculating…' The real Bess could be hard, as some of her surviving letters show, but the world was hard to her.

Portrait of Bess of Hardwick

NATIONAL PORTRAIT GALLERY

Hardwick before Bess

Bess was probably born in 1527 at Hardwick, where her family had lived since at least the thirteenth century. They took the name 'de Herdewyk' from their manor. It meant, literally, 'sheep farm'. In 1314, Robert, son of Jocelin de Hardwick, was sued for taking and detaining an ox.

The fact that there is no medieval walling incorporated in the Old Hall suggests that the Hardwicks built their house anew on the present site sometime in the sixteenth century.

This house survives as part of the Old Hall as it stands today: the south wall of the hall with its windows and perhaps the two storeys above it. Their medieval house was probably in a more sheltered position. A reference from 1570 to a 'first' house may refer to this medieval house, set back from the bluff edge, or it may mean that there were two buildings where the Old Hall now stands. This could explain the non-alignment of the two wings: perhaps they grew out of separate buildings. The scars in the hillside to the west below the Old

The ruins of the Old Hall, standing on the crest of the hill in front of the New Hall

Hall represent medieval terracing, walling, ploughing and fishponds.

A rent roll from 1570 describes the Hardwick family house. It was then owned by Bess's brother James. It had courts, barn yards and a dovecote yard. The remains of some of these buildings may lie beneath the lawn to the south of the Old Hall, where geophysical surveys have picked out the footings of walls. The survey goes on to mention various fields, woods, closes, pastures and fish ponds within the park. The rentable value of the house was set at 40 shillings, which suggests a building of some pretensions.

Bess' father died the year after she was born, leaving his wife and children in a quandary. As there was no adult male heir, the lands were forfeit to the Crown until the heir came of age. This was a survival of the custom that landowners had to provide service to the king as knights, and a boy under 21 obviously could not carry out this duty. By 1528, knights were no longer needed, but the custom was a useful way for the king to make money. Bess's father could only leave his 'childur' only £30 or £40 each.

Bess's mother Elizabeth had no choice but to remarry to provide for her children. Her second husband was Ralph Leche, who came from the family that owned Chatsworth. Her children by him, Bess's half-sisters, became Bess's closest

companions for the rest of her life. Mrs Knyveton, who had a room in the Old Hall, was one, and Mrs Digby was the daughter of another.

A rent roll listing the extent of the old Hardwick estate under James Hardwick, 1570

Bess herself was also expected to marry as a way out of these financial difficulties. She was no more than fifteen years old, and her husband, Robert Barley, was only thirteen. This was considered young even then, although a girl could be married from the age of twelve. But marriages would not be consummated until the bride was old enough to bear healthy children.

Only a year later, Robert died. Bess was left with a legal struggle to gain her share of his estate. Because he was under 21, there was the same trouble that land was forfeit to the Crown. Bess had to go out into the marriage market again, serving perhaps in the house of Lady Dorset. There she married Sir William Cavendish, her most loving husband, the one who gave her wealth and by whom she had eight children.

William Cavendish and William St Loe

Sir William Cavendish was a powerful courtier and a Privy Councillor. He had profited hugely from the Dissolution of the Monasteries and now made money from bribes – the normal way of doing business at court. He took Bess to live in London in a house just north of St Paul's where she had fifteen servants, for she was now a woman of importance. They lived in style, and were able to buy the Chatsworth estate from the Leche family. Frances,

Bess's first child, lived, but her second, Temperance, died. Her second son William, born in 1551, became her favourite and, as we have seen, later lived with her at Hardwick.

Sir William fell foul of the government soon after Queen Mary's accession in 1553. He was accused, correctly, of corruption, but the real reason was that he was too close to Mary's sister and rival, the Protestant future Queen Elizabeth. Sir William and Bess were both firm Protestants at a time when Catholics were in power. Faced with a huge fine, Sir William died. Bess was left owning a great deal of land, but also owing a great deal of money. 'I most humbly beseech the Lord to have mercy and rid me and his poor children out of our great misery', she wrote. She kept the little jewelled book that Sir William had given her with their two portraits in it until the end of her life.

Bess's friendship with Elizabeth paid off when Mary died in 1558. Bess came to court in a good position to look for another husband. She was only thirty, and soon attracted Sir William St Loe, the captain of Elizabeth's guard. Advanced in years, he seems to have been captivated by his young wife. 'My owne, more dearer than I am to myself' was how he began his letters to her, and 'Farewell, my own sweet Bess' was how he ended them. He did not live long but, much to the disgust of his family, left her lands in Somerset and

Gloucestershire. His brother had been involved in a sinister plot to poison Bess.

Bess's eldest daughter Frances married, by arrangement with the Pierrepont family of Holme Pierrepont near Nottingham. Frances was at least given the chance to see if she liked the boy on sight first. So she lived near to her mother's Derbyshire estates, and often sent across presents. Bess had started to rebuild her house at Chatsworth into a grand building. It was built in a different, less innovatory, style to Hardwick, simply but massively round a courtyard. In 1564 her husband wrote to her that he was glad of her good health, and that the sight of her newly-finished house would continue it.

While Bess was doing so well, her brother James, who had inherited Hardwick, was floundering. He seems to have been feckless, and many bonds

Chatsworth as rebuilt by Bess, before its eighteenth-century remodelling. Painting by Richard Wilson after Sibrechts

for his debts survive. He wrote to Bess asking for a loan: '£100 or failing that at least £50…I will pay whatever interest you will'. The loans and land sales gradually allowed Bess to get her foot into the door of Hardwick Hall.

Bess was in trouble at court at this time. She spent a spell in the Tower of London after being suspected of helping the queen's cousin, Lady Catherine Grey, make a secret marriage. Marriage was also a difficult and important issue for Queen Elizabeth. As Bess showed, it was the only way that a commoner could change her destiny. But a queen could only lose power by it. Elizabeth made great play of remaining always a virgin so as not to be dominated by a foreign prince. She was reluctant to let her ladies to marry, and once broke the finger of one of them in a fit of rage at a secret marriage.

Bess marries the Earl of Shrewsbury

But Bess was soon freed. She had been an early supporter of Elizabeth and was perhaps one of the people closest to being a friend to the queen. They even looked like each other, with their red hair. After the death of Sir William St Loe, as a rich widow in her late thirties, Bess could afford to pick and choose a husband. In the autumn of 1567, she married George Talbot, 6th Earl of Shrewsbury, one of the richest men in the country.

The merging of their great estates must have given the pair much satisfaction, for they also decided to merge their families. The Earl's son Gilbert and daughter Grace married Bess's daughter Mary, and her son Henry respectively. Bess's dynasty was henceforth to dominate the aristocracy of England, eventually linked to the dukedoms of Devonshire, Newcastle, Portland, Kingston and Norfolk. Bess's family even came close to becoming royal. Bess married her daughter Elizabeth into the Scottish royal family, and her granddaughter Arbella was a contender for the English throne.

The Earl of Shrewsbury seems at first also to have loved his wife. 'My jewel' and 'My own sweet heart', he wrote, thanking God that 'He hath sent me you in my old years to comfort me with all your comforts.' Life must indeed have been comfortable, with his houses at Sheffield Manor and Castle, Worksop Manor, Tutbury Castle, South Wingfield Manor, Rufford Abbey, Welbeck Abbey and Buxton Hall, and hers at Chatsworth, Hardwick (finally bought outright in 1583) and Oldcotes. In 1577 Bess wrote to thank her husband for the transport of some timber to Hardwick; perhaps some building work had already begun. The Earl was a keen builder and had constructed a great house at Worksop. He wrote to his friends about 'plattes' or plans for buildings.

George Talbot,
6th Earl of Shrewsbury

Partly because the Earl had so many houses and partly because of the trust she placed in him, Queen Elizabeth made the Earl the captor of Mary, Queen of Scots. She was a dangerous threat to the Crown, but also a costly drain on his resources and patience. Bess too was called upon to sit with 'the Scots Quene'. With his building projects and Mary's expenses, the Earl was running short of money, so in 1572 he signed a deed of gift. He gave Charles and William Cavendish the lands their mother Bess had brought to the marriage. This meant that he could avoid paying them the customary cash settlement on their coming of age. But this caused him trouble in the long run, for he needed the income from the lands he had given away. This explains the situation that led to Bess's return to her childhood home.

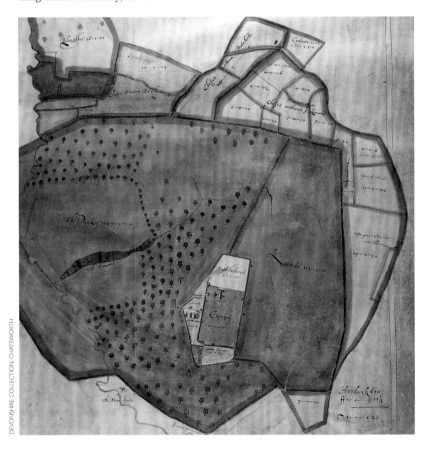

Part of William Senior's map of the Hardwick estate, 1610, showing the park divided into two.

War between the Earl and Countess

By the late 1570s the marriage was in difficulties. In 1577, her son-in-law wrote to Bess that the Earl was angry at her absence, but that he had not liked the household to see their differences and made excuses for her. By 1583 there was talk of arbitration of the financial dispute from outside, and the Earl accused Bess of setting her children to 'give evil speeches' against him. Rumours circulated that the Earl was too fond of his royal prisoner. Bess tried to look submissive in public, and may have even been unhappy in private. She wrote to a friend: 'I hope to find some friend for meat and drink, and so to end my life.' However, on 2 June 1583, she brought the Hardwick estate outright after her brother James had died a debtor.

The unhappy state of affairs continued. In 1584, the Earl reported to Sir Francis Walsingham (the Queen's secretary) that Bess had left Chatsworth, and carried off many things to the house of William Cavendish, her son, at Hardwick. Three years later, building work began in earnest to extend the old Hardwick family home, after a legal judgement had confirmed Bess's disputed allowance.

But Chatsworth had been bought for Bess by her second husband, Sir William Cavendish, and she was loath to give it up. It was hers for life. The Earl claimed it, and in 1584 the Privy Council heard how her son William Cavendish had repelled him with force. William was 'upon the leads with a halberd in his right hand', said the Earl. William defended himself by claiming simply that 'of habit [he] had always carried a pistol.' William was imprisoned for a time, even though he had the Earl's deed of gift.

'No curse or plague in the earth could be more grievous', wrote the Earl of the quarrel the next year, and feared that the queen was daily troubled by 'false reports' of him from his wife and children. Bess for her part kept up a diplomatically obedient attitude towards him in word, if not in deed: 'I will in all duty and humbleness subject myself to any other hammer of correction', she said, and the plaster scenes in the Old Hall Great Chambers may be part of this stance. But the Earl claimed she called him 'knave, fool, and beast, and mocked and mewed' at him.

The queen finally called the two before her and demanded a reconciliation. But local opinion was sceptical: 'In common opinion more likely were the wars in the Low Countries to take end than these civil discords between him and her.' And so it proved. The Earl was driven to accept the return of his wife, but would 'neither bed with her nor board with her'. A relative described how 'he saith he will rule my lady, but she saith little and plainly thinketh to govern him'.

Will:ᵐ Cavendishe
Earl of Devonſhire

Portrait of William Cavendish, Bess's favourite son, and future 1st Earl of Devonshire

Drawing of Oldcotes by the architect Robert Smythson. This was Bess's last house, built for her son William. Today nothing remains except part of the garden wall

So matters remained until the Earl, who had suffered for a long time from gout, died in 1590. Bess had enormous wealth, and enormous independence. Dealing with her royal grand-daughter, and building, occupied her for the rest of her life. Even before the Earl's death, Bess had started work on the stupendous New Hall. Even when it was finished, work continued at Oldcotes, expanding the house there into another residence for William. A payment was made in 1599 for 'the full fenyshing' of Oldcotes, despite disasters such as a collapse of a beamed ceiling there in October 1597.

Why did Bess have this mania for building? One reason is that it was a marvellous method of self-advertisement, symbolising her taste and wealth. As Francis Bacon wrote in 1594, 'when man sought to cure mortality by fame…buildings were the only way.' But Horace Walpole, the eighteenth-century antiquarian, gives another explanation. He describes a Cavendish family tradition that a fortune-teller had told Bess that 'she should not die while she was building: accordingly, she bestowed a great deal of the wealth she obtained from three of her four husbands in erecting large seats …

and died in a hard frost, when the workmen could not labour.'

True or not, she did die in an unusually frosty February. In 1607 she 'did eat very little and was not able to walk the length of the chamber', dying on 13 February 1608. The house where she was born, now much enlarged, was close by the new house where she died. As her descendant, the 6th Duke of Devonshire said, 'Bess's cradle must have been nearly as fine as her bed of state.'

Bess's descendants

The Halls were duly inherited by her son William, who was created 1st Earl of Devonshire in 1618. Accounts from his time show that the Old Hall was extended. John Smythson, the architect son of his famous father Robert, appears. His work may well have been the indoor tennis court that was added in 1619 to the western side.

The 1st Earl's own son William was tutored by the philosopher Thomas Hobbes. The 'Giants' Chamber' was the scene of Hobbes' experiments with his 'tube' and 'perspective glasses', the components of a telescope. He also used it, on a stand, in the newly fitted-out library in the Old Hall. In 1681 there were 65 servants at Hardwick, including three nursery maids, a helper in the laundry and 'ould Margery'.

By the eighteenth century, however, the Dukes of Devonshire preferred the rebuilt Chatsworth to unfashionable Hardwick. The Old

A Derby plate from the Regency period showing Old and New Halls

A bill from the builder William Bunting for two days' work in 1782 to prop up the roof of the 'Giants' Chamber'

Hall was partially demolished for the sale of its materials. In 1747, slates were taken to repair roofs elsewhere. The tennis court was pulled down in 1751. Most of the demolition was done in 1757 when £306 6s 9d was made in profit from 'Old House Materials at Hardwick sold', including 39 tons of plaster and 122.5 yards of wainscot. It is not clear why the south elevation was left. Certainly a little later it came to be seen as an attractive romantic ruin, such as appeared in the 'gothick' novels and art of the Picturesque movement.

The west wing survived. In 1782, the Giants' Chamber was examined and the roof propped up. In 1789, the tourist John Byng visited. He found the housekeeper of the New Hall living in the west wing. She was Elizabeth Brailsford, wife of the park keeper, and took him on a tour. He was allowed to root about in the abandoned library: 'I found myself amidst a large parcel of pamphlets, letters and accounts…some letters directed to the old Countess…which wou'd bear a hearty rummage.' In the same year there was also the 'shifting of things from the Old Hous' as part of the work carried out by the architect John Carr of York.

In the early nineteenth century gradual decay set in. The Hall began to appear in many romantic prints and engravings, some complete with storms and bats. The 6th Duke of Devonshire took a great antiquarian interest in his estates, and wrote about the Old Hall to his sister: 'This ruin is no longer so great a lion as it was once: it does not seem very safe.' He went on to tell the story of a risky

A nineteenth-century romantic engraving of the ruins

ascent to the roof of the Giants'
Chamber in 1816: 'Nicholas
Paulowitsch mounted upon it with
me. He took off his cap after his
descent, and, with an expression of
much thankfulness, made the house
a low bow. In 1832 the Princess
Victoria wanted to see the Giants'
Chamber, but I really thought it my
duty to say "Impossible, madam".'

The Giant's Chamber still had a
floor in the late nineteenth century
when photographed by Derby pho-
tographer Richard Keene, but decay
continued. The visitors who now
flocked to the site were part of the
problem. One nineteenth-century
travel writer described the more
unruly as 'fellows who richly merit a
flogging at the cart's tail', who had
'defaced many of the decorations by
scrawling on them'.

Visiting increased in the twentieth
century. The Duke of Devonshire's
accounts for 1954 include a payment
for 'washing down, re-writing and
fixing "Warning" notices to Ruin
Wall.' But once the estate was given
to the nation, a programme of con-

*A late nineteenth-century
photograph of the Hill
Great Chamber still roofed
and floored*

*The Old Hall seen from
the library of the New
Hall. Illustration from
Vitruvius Britannicus,
1835*

solidation took place which made the ruin safe to enter.

In the 1990s, the Hall was made structurally stable and the Hill Great Chamber partially refloored. Loose stonework has been recorded, repaired and the important plaster-work consolidated with soft lime mortars. The programme of work has continued with the restoration of the lodges and the tennis court yard, and will go on into the future.

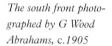

The south front photo-graphed by G Wood Abrahams, c.1905

DERBY CITY MUSEUMS AND ART GALLERY

FURTHER READING

Boynton, L. (ed.) *The Hardwick Hall Inventories of 1601,* Furniture History Society, 1971.

Durant, D. *Bess of Hardwick. Portrait of an Elizabethan Dynast,* Weidenfeld & Nicolson, 1977.

Durant, D. & Riden, P. *The Building of Hardwick Hall,* Derbyshire Record Society, 1983.

Girouard, M. *Robert Smythson and the Elizabethan Country House,* Yale, 1983.

Girouard, M. *Life in the English Country House,* Yale, 1983.

Wells-Cole, A. *Art and Decoration in Elizabethan and Jacobean England,* Yale, 1997.

ACKNOWLEDGEMENTS

Important archives are at Chatsworth, the Department of Manuscripts and Special Collections at Nottingham University and the Derbyshire Local Studies Library in Matlock. Thanks to Crick Smith Paint Research, John Cunnington Architects, David Durant and Ben Cowell of the National Trust.